A SHORT GUIDE TO THE ROMAN WALL

by T.H. Rowland, M.A.

TURRET NEAR CARVORAN

This engraving by C.J. Spence was published before this section of the wall was destroyed in 1883.

colour illustrations by R. Embleton

ISBN
0946928 266

Butler Publishing
Rothbury, Morpeth, Northumberland

Roman Officer's costume with muscle cuirasse

HADRIAN'S WALL

Hadrian's Wall must be listed among the most famous monuments in the world. It is a reminder of Roman imperial pride and defined, for a great part of the time that the Romans were in Britain, the northernmost limit of their Empire.

The Romans in expanding their Empire outwards from the Mediterranean found difficulty in defining frontiers — the effective limits of communication. In Britain the navy was of the greatest importance. The Emperor Claudius ordered the conquest of Britain from A.D. 43. He was not a prepossessing character and needed some great success — the crossing of the ocean and the conquest of another land. The southern parts were easily overcome, the north with greater difficulty. Agricola established a temporary frontier in the Tyne — Solway area and then pushed into Scotland, establishing a frontier on the Forth — Clyde.

In A.D. 85 he was recalled and in time the Romans returned to Agricola's old line of the Stanegate on which forts had been established. The loss of a legion meant that conquest and control were more difficult. The Emperor Hadrian came to Britain in A.D. 122 and decided upon the line of the Wall. This was from the Tyne to the Solway — the Emperor had an eye for a situation and he wanted to establish peace.

The original intention was for a wall of seventy-six Roman miles in length and built in stone from Newcastle to the River Irthing in Cumberland. It was to be ten feet wide and fifteen feet high. From the Irthing to the Solway there was to be a turf wall. In front of the Wall was a V-shaped ditch, nearly thirty feet wide and ten feet deep. At each mile there was a fortified gateway with a walled enclosure called a milecastle. This contained barracks and access to the top of the Wall. At intervals of one-third of a Roman mile were turrets, twenty feet square, which were used as watch towers.

The barrier was intended to divide the Romans from the barbarians to the North. A careful watch could be kept and unauthorized intrusion prevented. The gateways through the milecastles were to provide for civilian as well as military traffic — hence the large number of them, later to be reduced in size. It seems that the transit of people and animals was the main purpose of these, rather than any special military strategy. A group of at least twenty men would be necessary to keep a permanent watch. With turrets at one-third of a mile intervals one does not have to imagine a constant patrol along the top of the Wall. Enough could be seen from the lofty turret. It is not at all certain how the wall top was finished.

Additions were made in that the Wall was extended from Newcastle to Wallsend and a number of towers were added along the Cumberland coast. But changes were made during the process of construction.

The first was to move the forts up to the line of the Wall itself. Where the nature of the land allowed it, the forts were built astride the Wall, so that there were three gates of each fort to the north of the Wall to provide easy exit and entry for the troops. At Housesteads the fort was built with its north wall along the line of the main Wall and no northern ditch was needed because of the nature of the landscape.

Another change or addition was the construction of a ditch to the south of the Wall, the distance varying with the terrain. This is generally called the Vallum and consisted of a flat bottomed ditch about twenty feet wide and ten feet deep with wide platforms on either side, bounded by very pronounced mounds of soil taken from the ditch. This provided a very definite barrier to the south of the Wall, and it was intended to define the military area. The natives would be able to cross the Vallum at fixed points only opposite the gates to the forts. Traffic would be more strictly channelled.

There was still another change in the process of building, which took several years after A.D. 122. The construction of such a wall was an enormous task and vast quantities of stone had to be quarried. After it was decided to construct the forts on the Wall it was also decided to reduce the width of the unfinished Wall to seven and a half feet. This would save material and speed up the work – it explains the features of the Wall in parts, i.e. narrower wall on broad foundations and helps to date the building of different stretches of the Wall.

The Wall was built by the Roman soldiers. It was a skilled task and inscribed stones record the section of the army that did the building. The stone came from neighbouring quarries and possibly from the ditch in parts. Carefully cut stones provided the facing of the Wall and more irregular stones and lime cement provided the filling. It was a very substantial structure, but provided a ready quarry for stone robbers of later ages.

Modifications in plan explain some of the features that occur, but it also seems that legions might have built in a different style. There are three types of milecastle, differing in size and type of doorway. There is also some variation in the turrets.

Besides Housesteads, three other forts – Great Chesters, Carrawburgh and Carvoran were constructed behind the Wall. Carvoran was a Stanegate fort rebuilt in stone.

It would seem that the construction of a bridge over the Tyne at Newcastle was essential to the scheme of building from the earliest stage. Newcastle then had the name of Pons Aelii and was the key to the east end of the Wall. The other main crossing of the Tyne was at Corbridge. The Wall itself was carried by bridge over the North Tyne at Chesters and over the Irthing at Willowford Bridge, below the fort of Birdoswald. The turf wall originally constructed here was later rebuilt in stone.

The whole of the complex of frontier defences – the Wall ditch, Wall and Vallum – was the conception of the Emperor Hadrian and his friend, the governor Aulus Platorius Nepos, was responsible

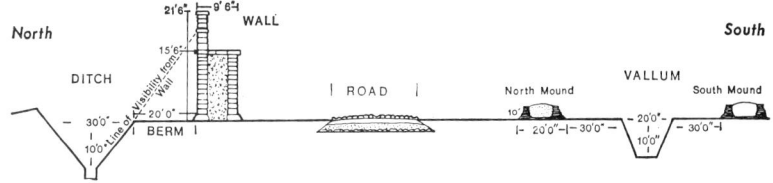

Cross Section of the Wall

for putting the scheme into effect. It was the work of the legions and the monument to a great builder.

After the death of Hadrian a change of policy meant the extension of the Roman frontier. Agricola's line of the Forth – Clyde was re-established and another wall was constructed here – the Antonine Wall. Hadrian's Wall was opened to let traffic through and the Vallum partly filled to allow passage to the North. The extension was not permanent and various troubles were experienced. After the turn of the century (A.D. 200), the Emperor Severus had to restore order in the North. He decided to repair Hadrian's Wall and this remained the Roman frontier with allied and protected territory beyond. After the Romans left, the Wall suffered from plundering and has provided material for building churches, farm houses and field walls. The worst destruction came in the middle of the eighteenth century after the 1745 Rebellion, when the Military Road was constructed from Newcastle to Carlisle. For many miles the Wall provided the foundations for the road and only isolated pieces remain. Antiquarians have attempted to appraise and preserve it and in modern times the Department of Environment protects and restores.

The Wall is best explored, as William Hutton did, on foot, and especially from Chesters westward. But all areas are worth exploring and none should be neglected. Towns, in particular, have material in museums, namely South Shields, Newcastle and Carlisle.

A SURVEY OF THE ROMAN WALL

The tendency is to follow the Wall from east to west – this is a matter of use and the fact that the Ordnance Map of Hadrian's Wall details Roman remains in this direction, starting with Milecastle 1 and another is located every Roman mile. The first turret is termed 1a and the next 1b, each separated by a third of a Roman mile. Milecastle 2 is followed by Turret 2a and then 2b. There follows Milecastle 3, Turret 3a and Turret 3b and so on. Every five miles or so is situated a Roman fort. The Ordnance Survey Map details all known Roman remains – those that are visible are shown in black, and it is essential to a proper investigation of the Wall.

In travelling from east to west *the Wall ditch* appears on the right hand to the north of the Wall itself. It was V-shaped, being

5

some twenty-seven feet wide and nine feet deep. It was separated from the Wall by a space of twenty feet wide called 'the berm'. The ditch was cut out along the entire length of the Wall, except when the Wall ran along the edge of a precipice.

The Wall itself started on a Broad foundation – ten feet wide but by a change of plan this was reduced to seven feet six inches wide, thus saving twenty-five per cent of material in building. In parts the Narrow Wall can be traced on Broad foundation and usually turrets and milecastles carry a short section of Broad Wall. In some places the Wall has completely disappeared especially in the Newcastle and Carlisle areas; elsewhere it may remain as high as fourteen courses. Behind the Wall was a Military Way linking the forts and leading to and from their east and west gates. It was about sixteen feet wide and it can still be traced. This is not to be confused with the Military Road constructed in mid-eighteenth century and for which the material of the Wall was used from Newcastle nearly to Chollerford (A69).

The Vallum lies to the south of the Wall at a varying distance depending on the landscape form, for it was not moved up to a higher level in hilly country. It is difficult to sort out on account of later fillings and re-excavations. Basically it was a flat bottomed ditch twenty feet wide and ten feet deep. The upcast was taken back on either side to a distance of thirty feet and piled in two parallel mounds twenty feet wide and six feet high. The total width of these earthworks was 120 feet.

After Hadrian's time the Vallum went out of use and at forty-five yard intervals the banks were breached and the ditch was filled. At a later stage the ditch was re-excavated and the spoils piled up on the margin. But in some parts this was not done and so the crossings can still be traced. There were obviously permanent crossings at the forts. The Vallum was to determine and control the military area.

The Forts had the characteristic shapes of playing cards with rounded corners. Each corner carried a defensive turret and there were defensive ditches. The forts were of two sizes – three acres as at Carrawburgh and Great Chesters or four and a half to five and a half acres as at Housesteads and Chesters. Most were so arranged that one-third of the fort projected beyond the Wall, but others like Housesteads lay entirely behind the Wall. The larger forts could take 1,000 infantry or 500 cavalry, the smaller 500 infantry. Forts were built to a similar plan whether marching camps with ditches, ramparts and timber palisades with tents inside, or forts built of timber or stone. There was usually a surrounding ditch and within this a stone wall five feet thick. There were four double gates, one set on each of the four sides and a single gate on each of the long sides. The via principalis linked the main side gates, the via quintana linked the single side gates. In the central area between these roads was the headquarters (principia). The via praetoria linked the north gate with the principia and the via decuma linked it with the south gate.

The northern third beyond the wall contained three gates, thus allowing easy entry and exit for the troops. In this area was a series of barrack blocks. The central sector contained granaries, workshops, the headquarters building and the commandant's house. The headquarters was an assembly area for various purposes, including the giving of instructions and the making of payments.

The other third contained further workshops and barrack buildings. These were set out in a regular pattern with sufficient space between the buildings themselves and the walls of the fort. The guard rooms at the gates and the towers on the walls had to be manned.

Outside the fort was usually a bath house and a civilian settlement. There were houses, gardens, shops, taverns and temples. Fields and terraces were cultivated. Beyond the fort and settlement areas were the burial places. There is usually some evidence of mining and quarrying. The Romans made use of any local resources.

A number of temporary camps or enclosures can be picked out in each area.

Reconstruction of a Milecastle.

7

The milecastles are a Roman mile (1,620 yards) apart. They were constructed early with thick walls, so the north wall linked with the Wall itself. The dimensions were something like sixty feet by seventy feet and the southern corners of the milecastle were rounded. There was a gateway, ten feet in width, through the Wall and a corresponding gate leading into the milecastle. On either side of the road was a long barrack building for the troops. Thirty-two soldiers could be housed and there was a flight of stone steps leading to the rampart walk. There were cooking facilities and stores within the milecastles. At a later date the gateways were much reduced in size.

The turrets are some twenty feet square and recessed into the Wall. There is one doorway leading into the turret, but not through the Wall. On the ground floor was a hearth and place to stand a moveable ladder leading to the turret top. It is likely that four men from the milecastle would occupy the turret and share duty, two by two, so that permanent watch could be kept upon the Wall.

Reconstruction of a Turret.

8

THE WALL BY STAGES

The mouth of the Tyne is a suitable place to begin, since this no doubt impressed Hadrian when he came. The river received Roman shipping and South Shields became an important supply base. Roman sailing ships anchored in the Tyne, bringing supplies. It is likely that smaller craft plied up and down the river.

South Shields fort (Arbeia) was a well chosen site, guarding the river mouth and checking the crossing of the Tyne. There may have been a fort in Agricola's time. Hadrian certainly built one and it was rebuilt in the time of Severus with a large number of store houses. Visible remains are part of the west wall and gate, the foundations of the granaries, barrack blocks, kilns and water supply. There is a small museum on the site and the material excavated from the fort is very well displayed, with cards explaining the making of articles and their uses. There is a fine tombstone to Victor the Moor and another to Regina, wife of Barates of Palmyra, who is shown sitting in her wicker chair. There is a dedication to Aesculapius, a god of healing and medicine. An inscription commemorated the provision of an aqueduct for the fort. A collection of gold and silver coins, enamel work and pottery are on display. Pride of place goes to the Roman sword, which is an early example of pattern welding and has golden bronze inlays on each side of the blade. The fort was connected to Chester-le-Street by the road called Wrekendyke.

Wallsend

On the north side of the Tyne was Segedum, now called Wallsend. This was not the original terminus of the Wall, but was at the end of an extension of the Narrow Wall (so later), taking in a great loop of the river. The fort was well placed on the higher ground and the Wall was continued to the river. It was probably extended to stop surreptitious crossings of the Tyne at low tide. Before modern building covered the area there was evidence of a large vicus or civilian settlement attached to the fort.

The area was extensively excavated, but there are no remains of the site. The fort, however, has been outlined in paving stones in the streets of the modern town. It covered four acres and had four double gates, three of them north of the Wall. There are some Roman antiquities in Wallsend Town Hall and some masonry from the Wall in the Park. Four milecastles have been traced between Wallsend and Newcastle, but the intervals were not regular.

Newcastle

The fort of Pons Aelii, the original end of the Wall, stood on the site of the Castle. Excavations have revealed Roman remains, but not the precise alignment of the walls. The Roman bridge was on the site of the present Swing Bridge. Its piers, through the ages, carried a series of bridges till the great flood of 1771. When the Swing Bridge was constructed a century ago, the wooden piles and foundation of one Roman pier were recorded. There were cutwaters in each direction against tide and river. Two altars to sea gods, Oceanus and Neptune, were recovered in dredging the river. These were erected by the VI Legion and are preserved in the Museum of Antiquities, situated within the quadrangle of the University of Newcastle.

A visit to this Museum is essential to the study and understanding of the Wall. It contains a contour reconstruction of the Wall for its entire length, showing the physical features and the siting of the forts, milecastles and turrets. The roads and supply lines are also shown. There are models of Roman forts, milecastles, baths and military equipment. A fine collection of altars, carved and inscribed stones are on display. Some of these have been repainted as in Roman times. Pottery and various utensils are on show with some ornaments and rings. Coins are exhibited and there is a selection of aerial photographs. A lot of Mithraic material has been collected, and a temple of Mithras has been reconstructed, within which visitors can recapture something of the eerie ritual of the Sungod slaying the bull to inspire his worshippers.

West of Newcastle, milecastles and ditches have been traced, but the first visible remains are at Benwell.

Benwell (Condercum)

This fort covered more than five and a half acres and occupied a magnificent situation. It is now entirely covered by a reservoir and housing, but it was excavated and buildings showed that it was first occupied by cavalry. The headquarters with underground strong room, the commandant's house, granaries and barrack blocks have been revealed and recorded.

Existing evidence is outside the fort — the Vallum that had to deviate to take in the area and the causeway across it. This is to be found at the bottom of Denhill Park Avenue. It is a natural causeway, left in cutting the ditch. Its sides are revetted in stone for strength to carry the road. The supports for the double doors of the gate have been revealed by excavation. The Vallum crossing is the only one that has survived and it is important in that it fixes the dimensions of the ditch itself.

There was a vicus associated with the fort and the remains of the temple of Antenociticus are preserved in Broomridge Avenue. It is small, measuring ten by sixteen feet internally with thick walls and an apse which contained the statue of the god. There are two altars on either side of the apse. Replicas are on the site, but the originals and the carved head of the native god are in the Museum of Antiquities.

The external bath house to the fort has not survived. The fort itself was astride the Wall, with three gates to the north for rapid sallies if such should be necessary.

At Denton Burn is the first stretch of the Wall to be visible. It has been excavated and is in the care of the Department of Environment. This is the original Broad Wall and has a turret (7b) incorporated in it. Two successive raisings of the threshold can be seen, the evidence of rebuilding at different periods. The turret measures about thirteen feet square internally and is recessed into the Wall.

For several miles the Wall disappears under the road, but at times the Wall ditch and Vallum can be traced to the north and south respectively.

Heddon-on-the-Wall

On approaching Heddon the Vallum can be seen very plainly and then a fine length of the Wall itself to the south of the road. This is about 100 yards long, consisting of a foundation of flagstones for the Broad Wall (nine feet seven inches). The facing stones and the core are clearly seen. A kiln constructed in the Wall was of a later period. Roman stone has been used for the building of the Church of Heddon-on-the-Wall, which dates back to Saxon times and has a fine Norman chancel.

From Heddon, the Military Road begins and to make it the Wall was flattened out. The Wall ditch is evident to the north and the Vallum to the south. Turrets and milecastles have been investigated but nothing is now visible.

The next Roman fort can be located at **Vindobala**, the cross-roads of **Rudchester.** It covers an area of four and a half acres and was originally a cavalry fort with three gates north of the Wall. Excavation has shown that the Wall ditch, dug before the fort was built, had to be filled in. The main west gate had been blocked at an early stage. Limited excavations have taken place in the area near the farm of Rudchester. The gates were located and the extent of the enclosure. The headquarters in the centre were investigated and a large granary. Much Roman stone has been used in the farm buildings and field walls. The part of the fort north of the road has been very much levelled by the plough, but irregularities in the field between the road and the farm show the main area of the fort. It is well situated at the top of a slope overlooking the Tyne valley. In the area of the civilian settlement was a structure once known as the "Giant's Grave". Perhaps this was the site of a Mithraeum from which five altars were recovered in the last century.

The Mithraeum was excavated in 1953 and revealed a stone building forty-three feet by twenty-two feet with an apse. It was built in the early third century, and there were stone benches on either side of the temple for reclining worshippers, who took part in a ritual feast. The temple was intended to be like a cave and there was usually a ritual pit for initiation ceremonies. The temple had been later rebuilt in a better style, but seems to have been deliberately destroyed in the Christian period. The heads of the attendants of Mithras, Cautes and Cautopates, usually shown with uplifted and

11

lowered torches to signify light and darkness, were discovered on excavation.

From Rudchester the landscape is more open on both sides. The old toll house at Rudchester has disappeared, like the Wall that disappeared when the road was constructed. Much stone has gone for the building of Welton Tower in the medieval period and the later Jacobean Hall attached to it. This can be seen in the area of the Whittledean reservoirs and a little beyond at the top of a rise is the site of Milecastle 17. The turrets here change – previous turrets have the door in the south-east corner and the ladder platform in the south-west corner. This is now reversed and the Wall itself differs a little in construction – three courses of stones between foundation, and offset instead of one, as before this.

In this part the earthworks can be traced and there is a particularly interesting section at Wallhouses. When the Antonine Wall replaced that of Hadrian, the Vallum was filled in at forty-five yard intervals to provide regular crossings. This left gaps in the mounds on either side of the Vallum. At a later stage when Hadrian's Wall was restored the Vallum crossings were dug out again and in subsequent recleaning the spoils were deposited on the margin of the ditch. At Wallhouses the ditch crossings were not removed and another feature at Matfen Piers is a small mound like a traverse obstructing the approach to each crossing. In this area the Wall ditch to the north of the road is very pronounced.

Milecastle 20 was at Halton Shields and the Vallum came close to it. At Down Hill there is a very good section of the Vallum. The gaps made in the mounds are plain, but the crossings of the ditch have been re-excavated. There are signs of very considerable Roman quarrying at Down Hill.

Halton (Hunnum) is the next fort. It is not easy to locate, since the area north of the road is almost completely levelled. There was very considerable stone robbing and Halton Tower (medieval) was constructed from Roman stone. A bath house within the fort to the north of the road was recorded by Hodgson. The present road passes through what were the east and west gates and covers the Wall itself. Excavations took place in 1936 and a building stone of the VI Legion, mentioning Nepos as governor, was discovered. The fort was originally for cavalry with three gateways to the north of the Wall. There had been a later extension of the fort to the west. An aqueduct brought in water from the source of the River Pont. There was a considerable civilian settlement in the neighbourhood of the fort. The road to the west has been investigated, and at the present time the approach road to the roundabout goes to the north of the Wall. A number of trial trenches along the old road have revealed the Wall beneath.

Near the present roundabout was Portgate – this permitted the main Roman road from south to north, Dere Street, to pass through the Wall. The road from further south came to Corbridge and then

Opposite: Roman Legionaries of the 2nd century with their packs.

penetrated the Wall, making its way to Newstead in Scotland. A branch road from this diverged at Bewclay and continued across country to the mouth of the Tweed. It is called Devil's Causeway.

Corbridge (Corstopitum) was situated two miles to the south and to the west of the present town. There was an Agricolan fort here on the Stanegate. This overlooked the crossing of the Tyne. The bridge was some distance west of the present bridge from which it can be approached by paths on either side of the river. The Roman bridge had stone piers and eleven openings. Some of the masonry can be seen in the river and there is a model of the bridge with its timber superstructure in Corbridge Museum.

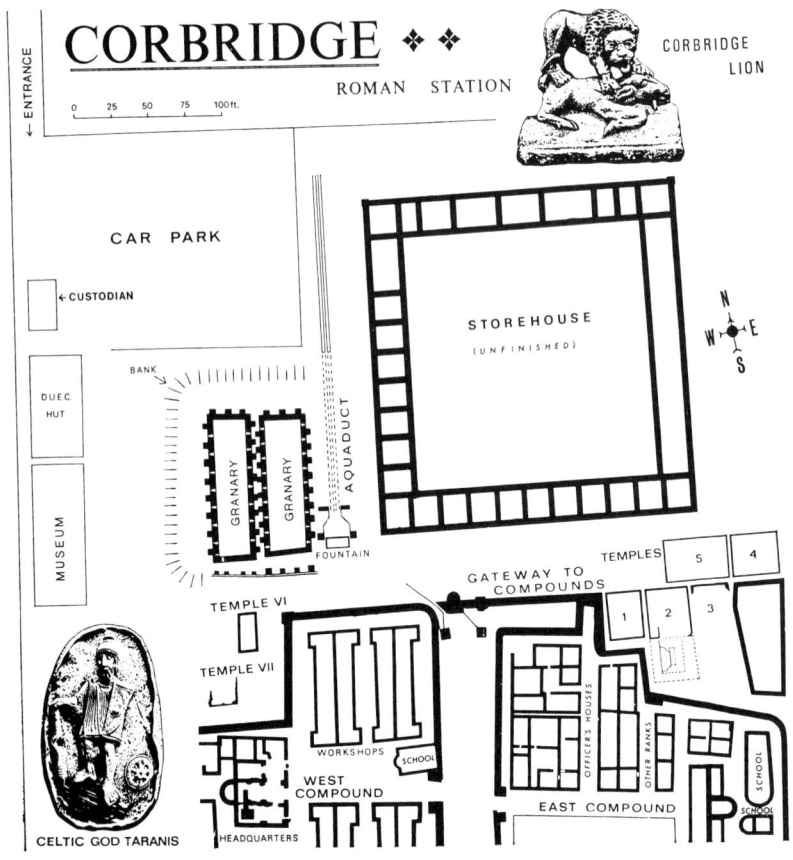

CORBRIDGE ❖ ❖

ROMAN STATION

CORBRIDGE LION

CELTIC GOD TARANIS

14

Corbridge, because of its situation on the river and the Roman main road, became the most important place in the area of the Wall. It still had use when the forts were moved to the Wall, and in time it became an important supply base on the route to Caledonia. It eventually became a small town covering some forty acres. The area now exposed is mainly that of the fort. The civilian areas are in the fields to the west and south of the fort. The bath house was situated nearer the river.

Corbridge is not an easy site to investigate and the visitor needs to keep referring to the plans in the Museum. A series of forts were superimposed and not on the same alignment. The earlier forts were of timber and in course of time were replaced by buildings of stone. These subsided over the ditches and the stonework that remains has a curious undulating effect. The buildings that remain are of the later period from the third century onwards. These include a massive storehouse compound that was not completed. There are two large granaries with ventilated basements and buttressed walls that had to carry a fireproof roof. The pillars of a colonnade are also visible, and the roadways of the fort. There were two special military compounds walled off, each having separate blocks and offices. These were used by craftsmen skilled in making and repairing military weapons and equipment. Some Roman armour has been found buried at Corbridge and many of the finds are kept in the Museum.

Of special interest is the water supply brought down to the site from the north by aqueduct. It fed a great stone cistern in the centre of the fort. The fountain head was the famous sculptured lion, shown with its prey. Much of the stone of Corstopitum has been used for building modern Corbridge. The church contains a complete Roman archway and much of the tower is built of Roman stone. Corbridge is regularly used as an excavation centre, and every summer areas of it are explored at different depths. Old timbers have been discovered and evidence of native dwellings before the Romans took over the site.

Returning to the Portgate on the Military Road, a very fine length of the Wall ditch is evident. In summer it can be magnificent with the sun shining on the golden gorse that fringes it. On this stretch, too, the Vallum appears very plainly. William Hutton when walking the Wall was amazed and "forgot I was upon a wild common, a stranger and the evening approaching. . . . lost in astonishment I was not able to move at all".

One section of the ditch, as noticed by Hodgson, shows the spoils, almost as they were tipped by the workmen.

There is much evidence of quarrying and, on Fallowfield Fell, Flavius Carantinus, a soldier, cut his name in the rock. This has been removed to Chesters Museum for preservation.

On the roadside is a wooden cross, marking the battle site of Heavenfield, where in 634 Oswald, the Christian king of Northumbria,

defeated Cadwallon, the pagan king, and avenged Edwin's death. Bede mentions that a Saxon Church was built there. The present church, to the north of the Wall, contains a Roman altar.

Further west at **Planetrees** is a piece of the Wall preserved by William Hutton in 1801. He pleaded with the farmer, who was using Roman stone for building, to spare this piece and it happens to contain a junction between the Broad and Narrow Walls.

After descending the hill it is worth while turning along the Hexham road to see **Brunton Turret.** Here the Broad Wall stands to the height of nine feet as far as the turret. This measures twelve feet nine inches by eleven feet six inches. It has been well preserved. The Wall to the east is narrow. In front of this section of the Wall is a good length of the ditch.

The Wall continues to the North Tyne at **Chesters.** A path can be followed, parallel to the old railway from Chollerford Bridge to the Roman bridge crossing the river. The Wall emerges as Narrow on Broad foundation, terminating with a twenty-two feet square tower on the bridge abutment. The bridge had three piers and could take a roadway of twenty feet. Investigations have shown that in Hadrian's time the piers carried only the Wall over the river, but at a later date a road was carried too. The arches of the bridge were probably closed by gratings to prevent entry. There was also a mill race at the eastern abutment, providing power for a corn mill in the tower. The stone hub of the water wheel as well as millstones are preserved in Chesters Museum. Roman columns from Chesters were used in the building of Chollerford Church, which is near, and there is a good deal of Roman stone embodied in Hexham Abbey.

Cilurnum. Chesters fort is approached by the Military Road beyond Chollerford and is under the care of the Department of Environment. It is beautifully situated by the river, in pleasant pastures protected by trees. In many ways it is the most rewarding fort to visit, although only part of it is exposed to public view.

A perambulation can be made round the perimeter of the fort to discover the shape and extent. It is shaped like a playing card with rounded corners, each taking a watch tower. The six gateways can be located — three to the north of the Wall. The junction of the Wall and the fort can be seen. In the north-east corner barrack blocks and stables have been uncovered, showing the accommodation.

In the centre of the fort is the principia or headquarters building. This was an assembly area for the troops. It consisted of a paved courtyard with porticoes on three sides. On the south side was a large hall with a rostrum or platform for the speaker. There was a series of five chambers, the central one being the regimental chapel for the keeping of the standards. The rooms on either side were for the keeping of records and pay. There is a vaulted strong room underneath.

Opposite: Stone Mason's Workshop.

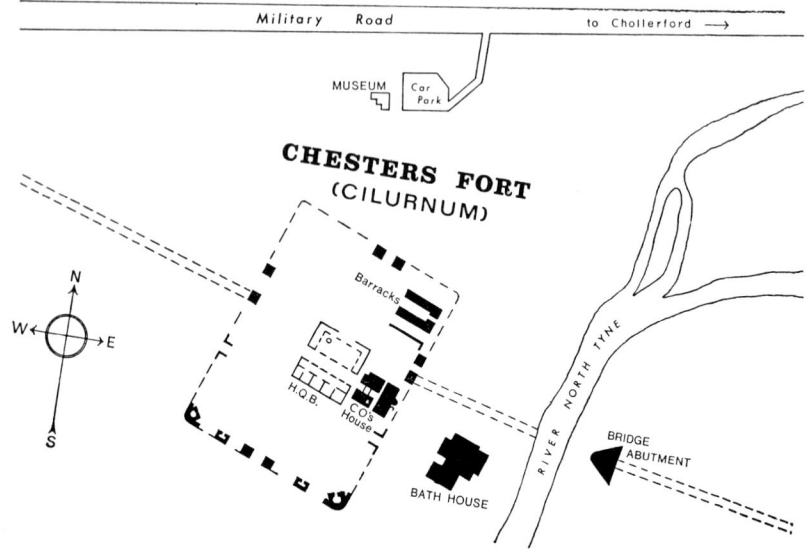

CHESTERS FORT
(CILURNUM)

MUSEUM   Car Park

Barracks

N
W←   →E
S

H.Q.B.   C.O's House

BATH HOUSE

RIVER NORTH TYNE

BRIDGE ABUTMENT

Adjacent to the headquarters was the commandant's house, with a full set of apartments centrally heated. The hypocaust or underfloor heating is seen with pillars to allow the circulation of hot air.

To the south of the fort was a large civilian settlement as revealed by air photography, and close to the river is the military bath house. This is particularly well preserved with fine stonework. It was plastered in Roman times. The bath-house was a social centre and perhaps used by civilians as well as the military. Refreshments were provided and games of chance took place. A small porch leads into a large changing room with wall cupboards. The latrine was on the river side, the furnace on the fort side of the building. There were a series of cold, warm and very hot rooms. In the hot room the bathing process was sweating, washing and scraping. There were hot wet and hot dry rooms and the return process was by warm and cold rooms to complete the circle. Water was brought down from the north to the fort and there was a settling tank in the north guardroom of the west gate of the fort. This supplied the barracks and finally the baths. The Romans were very particular about water supply and sanitation.

At Chesters the Clayton Memorial Museum contains a very fine collection of Roman material excavated or acquired by John Clayton. At one time he owned five Wall forts — Chesters, Carrawburgh, Housesteads, Chesterholm and Carvoran — and various finds from these places are included. There are a number of inscribed stones and a collection of altars. On display is a considerable amount of sculpture including the god of the Tyne, water nymphs and goddesses. The exhibits are rather overcrowded but repay a close scrutiny,

18

especially the sides of the altars. Pottery and glassware are shown in cases, together with small ornaments and utensils. There is quite a large collection of millstones and a large bronze corn measure which came from Carvoran. To some extent the imagination is able to reconstruct Roman buildings and their furnishings. Their axes, hammers, planes and entrenching tools are on display giving a good impression of the high level of Roman technology. Fragments of painted plaster and ornamental capitals give some hint of the interior of buildings of which only foundations remain.

The foundations of the Wall remain under the fields and gardens of the country house of Chesters and then under the road which rises past Walwick. At one time the Wall could here be seen in the road, but now reposes below a cover of tar macadam. Where the road leaves the Wall, the platform of Milecastle 28 can be picked out. The road climbs again past Tower Tye, a cottage constructed from Roman stone before the Military Road was made. Here Milecastle 29 has been completely robbed. The Wall was also robbed, but in the area of Black Carts, a length of Wall half a mile in length is exposed. It was excavated by Clayton and again became overgrown, but it is now in the protection of the Department of Environment. The vegetation has been removed and the stonework strengthened. Turret 29b is in this length of Wall, and a further stretch is being exposed to the west. The Wall ditch is plainly visible and from the top of the hill at Limestone Corner this long length of Wall can be viewed. There is a fine stretch of countryside to the north, which includes Chipchase Castle and Nunwick. Beyond lies the valley of North Tyne and the moorland reaches to the Cheviots.

At Limestone Corner the Wall again coincides with the road. There is a very fine section of both the Vallum and the Wall ditch as far as Carrawburgh. The ditch is well pointed and deep; the Vallum and both its mounds are very plain. At the corner these military works were cut into solid rock of the Whin Sill and were never completed. The outline of Milecastle 30 can be seen between the field wall and the road wall. Great blocks of stone were cut in both the ditch and Vallum. Some have been hauled out and left lying on the brink, others remain in the ditch. It seems that some official, recognising the incredibly hard labour involved, called it a day and the evidence has remained for hundreds of years. More modern wall and road builders left the huge rocks lying. The procedure for the Romans was to split the rock with wedges and raise the blocks by crane.

In this area too the Vallum crossing to the milecastle can be discovered. To the east is an area of the Vallum showing temporary crossings, to the west is an area unaltered by such fillings. The farm of Carrawburgh contains a good deal of Roman stone and to the west of it is the fort — Brocolitia to the Romans.

Carrawburgh fort is to the south of the Wall entirely and it is considered to be later in date since the Vallum was partly filled to

A Mithraic Ceremony.

provide the necessary space for it. The north wall of the fort coincided with the Wall and it was constructed to fill in the long gap of more than eight miles between Chesters and Housesteads. The fort is situated on a low eminence and the outline of it can be determined, but much of the stonework has been robbed. Some excavations have recently taken place in the area of the headquarters and the granaries have been located.

There are indications of a civilian settlement, but the most interesting sites are the **Mithraeum** and Coventina's well. The Mithraeum was revealed in the drought of 1949, which caused shrinkage of the peat and three altar tops emerged. The temple was excavated in 1950 by Professor Ian Richmond and the report is a model of its kind. The Mithraeum was built in the third century for the worshippers of the Persian sun god – a select group of men from the army. The building was in stone and modified several times before destruction in Christian times. The door leads to an ante chapel, where ritual meals were prepared, and an ordeal pit for initiation. A wicker screen supported by posts divided this from the nave, on either side of which were wicker benches for worshippers. Three altars were at the far end (replicas are now in place), and a relief showing Mithras slaying the bull. The temple has been preserved, but much of the material was taken to the Museum of Antiquities.

The bath-house was excavated by Clayton in 1873, and some miners looking for lead discovered Coventina's well. This proved to be a shrine about forty feet square in the centre of which was the well of the water goddess. At some time in confusion from an attack, the ornaments, coins and containers were thrown into the well. Clayton recovered 13,847 coins of various types and others were stolen. There were carved stones, altars, incense burners and brooches thrown into the well. The coins were mostly bronze. This neglected site is water-logged and overgrown with rushes – it might be restored to attract more modern well wishers.

Three miles to the south at **Newborough** is another fort on the Stanegate. Continuing westwards the Wall ditch and Vallum are still visible and the site of Milecastle 32. There are two Roman camps traceable in this area. Milecastle 33 is at Shield-on-the-Wall. To the south of the road is the reservoir for Settlingstones Old Mine and beyond to the west can be seen the terraces of the Whin Sill at Sewingshields and further. The Wall, which has been covered by the road, emerges to the north and so does the Vallum. This is quite a dramatic spot and earthworks are seen in both directions. Turret 33b (Coesike) has recently been excavated and remains exposed to view.

At Sewingshields a castle once existed and according to ancient story King Arthur, his Queen and Court, lie enchanted, awaiting the rousing blast of the horn which a hesitant shepherd failed to sound. A centurial stone is preserved in the walls of the farm and from the summit of Sewingshields can be seen the old earthwork called Black Dyke. Further west an old drove road passes through Busy Gap and on top of King's Hill is Milecastle 36. The Wall is reduced to a field wall, but a length of full width goes down to the Knag Burn Gate. This was one of the few gates through the Wall which were not at forts or milecastles. It was for civilian traffic and is overlooked by Housesteads Fort. The passage had guard houses at either side and pivot holes show that there were two sets of doors, so that people could be checked by customs or security officials either way. The Knag Burn passes through a culvert in the Wall and supplied extra water for the Romans at Housesteads.

Housesteads (Vercovicium), is the most visited of the Roman forts on account of its magnificent situation. It is also provided with an extended car park, and the site can be first surveyed from a distance. The fort is on the crest of the Whin Sill — the slope faces the sun and receives some shelter. It is seamed with cultivation terraces and the remains of a collection of houses and shops of a large civilian settlement are visible. Since Housesteads provided for 1,000 troops it has been suggested that the civilian population was more than 2,000. It requires a good deal of time for the walk there and back, a look at the Museum and a full inspection of the fort. There are extended walks along the Wall either way.

On the way to the fort and beyond the fence at the bottom of the hill, is Chapel Hill where John Hodgson excavated the Mithraeum. There were a number of temples in the area and altars have been found. Some of the stones are preserved in the Museum, which was itself constructed from Roman masonry and planned to be the same size as a civilian house.

One of the civilian houses to the south of the fort is known as Murder House. During excavations two skeletons, one male and the other female, were found buried beneath the floor. They met violent

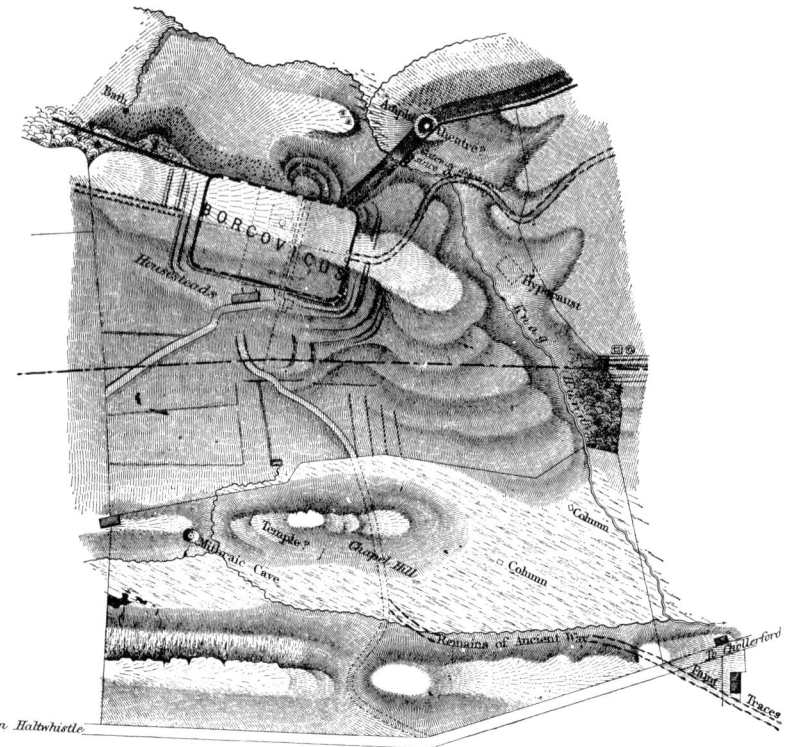

From MacLauchlan's map of the Roman Wall, 1861.

deaths and a normal burial would have been in a proper cemetery. The Romans were very particular about the siting of burial places and they usually provide valuable information, whether pagan or Christian.

The visitor has to pay the custodian at the Museum, so this may well be inspected first. It was constructed from Roman stone and opened in 1936. It contains models of the fort and a civilian house. There are sculptured stones and altars together with various examples of Roman material. Particularly interesting is the carving of three hooded deities, wearing the equivalent of "duffle coats". It gives an impression of a harsh climate, but in Roman times it was probably milder and the fort and Wall provided shelter from the blast. The Romans no doubt had adequate heating.

The fort is approached through the south gate, where one guard-room was later converted into a border tower and then a kiln for drying corn. The unusual feature about the fort is that it all lies behind the Wall with its long axis running east and west to a length of 610 feet. The north-south dimension is 367 feet. The fort has been aligned differently to meet the requirements of the landscape. Normally part of the fort was constructed to the north of the Wall, but here after the Broad foundation had been laid and a turret constructed the north wall of the fort replaced this.

The foundations of the turret can still be seen. The junction of the fort wall and the Wall itself to the north-east was not well contrived. This is a good point for making a survey of the country to the north, the Knag Burn and the layout of the fort itself to the south.

The north gate was approached by an embanked road, but this has been removed by excavators to expose the magnificent structure of the double portals in fine masonry. The eastern portal had been blocked and the level of the western portal had been raised. The guard chambers are still in good condition and outside was a large stone water tank for the collection of water and much worn by weapon sharpening. Since water could not be led from higher ground it was necessary to collect all possible from the roofs of the various buildings. If this failed water had to be raised from the Knag Burn.

To the east of the road between the north and south gates were a series of six long barrack blocks aligned east to west. The east gate had two portals, but the south portal was blocked and converted into a guard chamber. The old guard-room was converted into a coal store, where John Hodgson's excavators found nearly a cart load of local coal. The threshold of the gate is worn by the wheels of chariots and the wheel gauge was the same as British Railways. It shows that a similar width for carts had existed for centuries and this same width continued for wagonways and railways.

In the south corner of the eastern sector the latrines were situated, in such a way as to receive running water from higher cisterns. There was a long rectangular building in stone with two parallel sewers over which seating was arranged. A stone channel

23

between the rows contained water for the washing of cleansing sponges. It is a good example of Roman sanitation.

In the centre of the fort is the principia or headquarters, rebuilt in the time of Severus. This area has been recently re-excavated and the stonework is being consolidated against the weather by the Department of Environment. The arrangement is similar to Chesters but the remains are not in such good condition. Some 800 arrowheads were found in one room. The standards were stored in the chapel: pay and records of payment were kept here too. It was the administrative centre of the fort.

To the south was situated the commandant's house and there was also provision for a hospital. North of the principia were the two great granaries. These were strongly built and the stone supports for the timber joists are still there. The purpose was to take the great weight of the grain and allow free circulation of the air. The corn drying kiln here discovered by Hodgson was later than Roman date. Officials kept a check on what corn was taken in and distributed to the troops.

The western portion of the fort was occupied by barrack blocks, none of which are now visible. The west rampart stands eleven courses high and the west gate also stands high. It is worth completing the circuit outside the walls of the fort as well as examining the interior. Then time should be found, even if there is no intention of walking far, to complete the stretch westwards to Milecastle 37. This has been several times excavated and is in a state of good repair. It has walls nine feet thick and on either side the Broad Wall can be seen tapering to the Narrow. The north gate was originally ten feet wide and from this and existing masonry a height of fifteen feet has been calculated for the height of the rampart of the Wall. The door was reduced like others in the time of Severus to four feet. The most valuable relic from this site was an inscription commemorating the building of the original milecastle in Hadrian's time by the Second Legion under Aulus Platorius Nepos. It contained two barrack buildings. The Roman service road can be traced to the West gate of the fort and the Vallum can be seen both to east and west. Below the south wall of the fort the Vallum was obliterated by the civilian settlement. There were cultivation terraces on the slopes and there are fine views towards the Tyne valley. Roman quarries can be recognised in the area and there was a good deal of limestone working.

Vindolanda has taken up its Roman name and is sign-posted thus. It carried the name of Chesterholm and the change is a symbol of most interesting developments. In the past the Roman Wall has been considered from a military point of view with problems of strategy and the use of the troops. Although it was known that each fort had a civilian settlement connected with it, this aspect has not been considered a great deal until recently. Mr. Peter Salway made a survey of civilian sites, using aerial photographs as a basis. Vindolanda is the first to be thoroughly investigated by Mr. Robin

Birley, Director of Excavations. The site has been placed in the care of a Trust and excavations are being planned on a long term basis, making continual use of school parties. Already a great deal has been uncovered and a visit is strongly recommended as a contrast to the military sites.

However, Vindolanda must first be considered as a fort. It is situated two miles south of Housesteads and was one of the original forts on the Stanegate, which can easily be followed. On the approach to Vindolanda by the farm track, below the present car park, a mound appears to the right beyond the stream. This was an ancient tumulus or burial mound and under its shadow is a Roman mile-stone in its original situation. Another, a Roman mile to the west, has been removed. The fort is situated on a natural plateau, protected on every side except the west where the civilian site was. It was excavated by Professor Birley and presented to the nation by him. The area covered was three and a half acres and only the gateways to the north and west had guard chambers. These have been exposed and the headquarters buildings were also investigated. The remains are

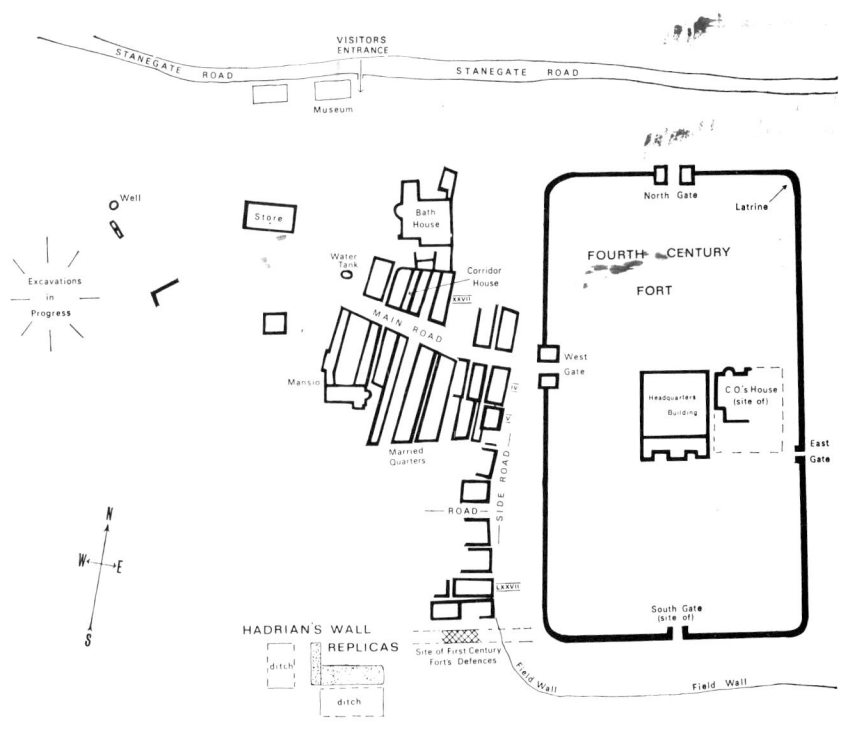

Vindolanda Camp and Vicus   Courtesy of Vindolanda Trust

25

now very well preserved. To the south are the administrative rooms with the Chapel of the Standards in the centre and the strong room for pay and savings underneath. The pairs of rooms on either side were used as offices. The cross hall contains the rostrum from which officers could address contingents of their troops. There is a well sunk down to bed rock in the courtyard, from which various objects were recovered. The rubbish of one age is the evidence for another. The north-eastern angle has recently been excavated and reinforced, but the main developments have been upon the civilian site. The approach is by the museum where selections of the finds are on display and relevant literature can be purchased including the latest guide to the site. This is produced annually, so much can be discovered in one year of excavation. There is continual work on the site — excavation, preservation and evaluation of the discoveries.

The visible remains on the site tend to be of the later period of Roman occupation and evidence indicates that people continued to live here after the Roman period. Items in the museum seem to indicate a fairly high standard of living in the civilian settlement.

The first building to be approached from the museum entry is the military bath-house. This was used by civilians and a number of female ornaments have been found in the drains. The bath-house is being put into a state of consolidation. There was plaster still on the walls at the time of excavation and there was a good deal of soot underneath, deposited by the furnaces for heating and the hypocaust pillars were blackened. The semi-circular wall enclosed the hot plunge bath and the other apartments are very similar to Chesters with changing room, cold, warm and hot rooms in sequence. Near the baths are a number of buildings including both houses and shops. One, a corridor type house, had three rooms on each side of a passage.

The main road, paved with large flat stones, leads direct to the west gate of the fort and on the south side of it were a series of military married blocks and a mansio or hotel for travellers. This consisted of a long courtyard with fifteen rooms or apartments spaced about it, which included kitchen, dining room and baths.

Further buildings of the third and fourth centuries have been uncovered between the west gate and the south-west angle of the fort.

The water supply has been traced coming in from the west and several water tanks have been uncovered. There is still a considerable area to be investigated and in course of time different levels of occupation from Agricola's time to the post-Roman period will be considered. It was a well chosen site for a settlement and a detailed survey of the entire area is worth considering with water supply and available building material. There were also local coal supplies.

Another feature at Vindolanda has been the construction of a replica of the Roman Wall. It has been the policy of the Department of Environment in this country to preserve and not to rebuild ancient remains. Here the Vindolanda Trust has undertaken some construction work on a part of the site that is free from Roman remains. A section of stone wall has been built from Roman stone from the site. It is ten Roman feet wide, fifteen Roman feet to the rampart walk and then a six feet parapet. It is a revelation to see the Wall at its full height.

Alongside is a section of the turf wall as originally built in Cumberland. This is twenty feet wide and rising to the same height as the stone Wall, but carrying a timber parapet. The work has been carried out by strong parties of school students under expert supervision. It is a practical study of the problems involved and adds to the interest of the site. Both sections of the Wall are fronted by a ditch, thirty feet in width and ten feet in depth – illustrating further the amount of work involved. It is hoped to construct a replica turret from which the whole of the area may be surveyed from a height. The intention also is to construct a new museum in the form of the headquarters building in which a rapidly increasing amount of Roman material can be put on permanent display.

By chance in 1972 another important discovery was made in the area of the south-west corner of the fort. A land drain was being laid and an original Roman turf rampart was revealed, but even more important this had sealed and preserved rubbish deposited before Hadrian's time. Middens and rubbish dumps often provide valuable evidence for the archaeologist. Some things survive – potsheards, stones, bones, shells and glass, but a lot of things perish rapidly, especially materials. Here was deposited a large quantity of leather and this had been preserved by water and had protected what was beneath. Cloth, hair, feather, dried bracken, manure, mosses, ferns and seeds were recovered. These were available for study by experts.

The leatherwork included a conical hat, an arm purse, pieces of tent walls and something like forty boots and shoes for men, women and children. One woman's sandal had the maker's name and trademark on it. The cloth fragments included one with a herringbone pattern.

Other things discovered on the site recently are the head of a Roman military standard showing a horse treading upon a snake. There is the bronze figure of an old man in a toga. In a storehouse was found an altar decorated with two staring eyes. The altars give some idea of the variety of gods, goddesses and spirits to which the Roman troops paid tribute. One was "To the God Moguntis and the genius of the place". Another was to the god Maponus.

Among the collection of finds are beads and gemstones, glassware, glass from windows, large storage jars, cooking pots, bronze from weapons and fittings, lead bullets for slingers, and millstones. There are many coins, hair pins and combs. Many aspects of life are revealed in some detail.

Still more things are coming to light – the latest are Roman documents in cursive script, preserved under the bracken of a first century barrack block. This rubbish was protected by the clay floor of a timber building and some slag from a Roman metal workshop. A lot more Roman cloth and leather has been discovered. These finds are now in process of preservation and investigation.

Housesteads is a good base for exploring the Wall – a bus or car can be parked for walking in either direction and returning. It has to be remembered that the distance is greater than appears, because of the undulating nature of the landscape. The wall itself is affected, because not only does it rise and fall but deviates to the north or south with breaks in the Whin Sill. The Romans had a point of entry on the lower ground covered from the Wall on either side and the ditch was also dug across the gaps.

Observing these features, the way the Wall was built on sloping ground and the junctions of different lengths of building, adds interest to the journey. The Wall itself sometimes disappears into a field wall.

Magnificent views can be obtained in all directions from **Cuddy's Crag,** though on a windy day it can be very wild. Housesteads and Sewingshields Crags rise to the east, with Broomlee Lough beneath. Greenlee Lough lies to the north and Crag Lough to the west. They are the haunts of waterbirds and on occasion geese or swans fly across. Further north the hills and forests and moorland wastes can be seen. There are scattered farmsteads beneath and from the height sheep and cattle look very small. Jackdaws haunt the rocks and the tenacious rowan trees cling to the crags. Mountaineers use the cliffs for their training. To the south lie the tree sheltered hollows of the Tyne valley and westward are the hills of Cumberland. The landscape can be exciting under a mantle of snow, when all kinds of features are etched in black and white. Cloud forms appear with dramatic effects. In mid-March and September the sun rises and sets directly over the line of the Wall.

Beyond Housesteads the Wall drops and rises to *Cuddy's Crag.* Then come Rapishaw Gap and Hotbank Crags. Turret 37a was not rebuilt under Severus, but there is a fine stretch of Wall preserved on the Crags, where the height above sea level reaches 1,074 feet. The Vallum tends to turn sharply southwards. The remains of the Wall end on the slope near Hotbank Farm, but Milecastle 38 can here be recognised. Here were found two inscriptions mentioning the Second Legion. The way out from the farm passes through the native settlement of Milking Gap, and a little way beyond this the main road runs for more than a mile along the Vallum. They diverge again beyond Twice Brewed and the Vallum turns north.

Beyond Milking Gap for a stretch the Wall has disappeared with turrets 38a and b, but the majestic cliffs and *Crag Lough* provide some compensation. In the next gap a section of Wall shows the difficulties of construction on sloping ground. There is another rise and fall, and in the hollow is Castle Nick (Milecastle 39), measuring sixty-two feet from north to south and fifty feet from east to west. The gateways were built of small stones. There is yet another crag and a gap called Cat Stairs. By descending this a striking view can be obtained of the crags from beneath. The Wall rises on Peel Crag, where it is preserved for some distance. Then in the very steep drop to Peel Gap the Wall has disappeared, but the Wall ditch was dug on the lower ground. On the western side of the Gap the Wall is preserved and turns north to Steel Rigg Car Park. The Wall stops at the road, but the ditch continues on the other side towards Winshields. There is a road leading south to Twice Brewed and northwards towards the scattered farmsteads.

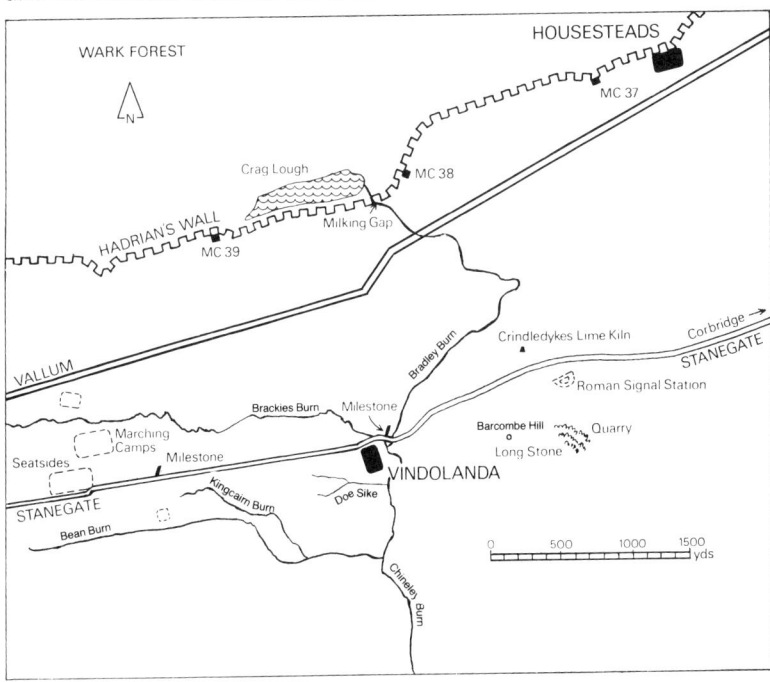

Continuing to follow the Wall up **Winshields Crag,** a magnificent view eastwards can be obtained showing the Crags and the Loughs. Westwards the Wall ditch continues up the slope and then the foundations of the Roman Wall appear beneath the field wall. Hereabouts is the site of Milecastle 40, similar in size to Castle Nick (more than 1,800 yards away). On Winshields Crags a fine stretch of Wall has been preserved and the highest point is 1,230 feet above sea level. More than thirty farmsteads can be distinguished with fields and approach roads, and looking westwards the Wall can be seen as far as Walltown Crags. Greatchesters can be picked out and the Vallum. Either way the Wall rises dramatically over the crags. A section of the Wall is well preserved, but it tends to merge with a field wall. In a sheltered hollow called Green Slack may be signs of a native settlement and before Lodham Slack the Wall again is standing on Broad foundation. The Wall ditch has been cut to the north.

Turret 40b appears on the next ridge and at a distance of 1,850 yards from the previous milecastle is Melkridge (Milecastle 41). The outline can be picked out in the turf and there seems to be an extra enclosure beside it. Here the Vallum has come much closer to the Wall and from the Crags it is very plain. The farm of Shield on the Wall stands almost on the south bank of the Vallum. An approach road comes in and makes for Cawburn. The Wall continues to the west of the road – it has been exposed and preserved by the Department of Environment. Since the stone was mostly covered it is in very good condition. The foundations of a Turret (41a) have been revealed with Broad Wall wings. When this section is completed there will be a continuous stretch of Wall to the margin of Cawfields quarry. The Wall ditch appears in the Caw Gap, and the Vallum can be distinguished. The Wall itself follows the cliff and rises and falls with the undulations. There is a particularly interesting section covering a gap called Thorny Doors, with a modern field gate. At one point the masonry stands fourteen courses high and it is carefully constructed against the slope. There is a sharp bend on the other side of the gap and the Wall re-occupies the edge of the cliff. Here again are extensive views. Two offsets can be seen in the Wall and Turret 41b has completely disappeared. The Wall continues to Milecastle 42, **Cawfields.** Some difficulty was caused by construction on a slope but the walls are strongly built – eight feet in thickness. It measures forty-nine feet from north to south and sixty-three from east to west. Both gateways are constructed in massive masonry and the north wall was built on Broad foundation. On either side of the milecastle can be seen the points of reduction. It was built by the Second Legion and a Hadrianic inscription has been discovered. The Wall falls sharply to a farm gateway and then rears to the point of disappearance over a precipice. This is Cawfields Quarry – responsible for the removal of the rock above and below. The area is being converted into a County Park and Picnic Area by the levelling of quarry spoils. The Caw Burn flows swiftly past, but the site of a Roman Mill has disappeared. The line of the Wall can be detected leading across to the fort of *Greatchesters*. A road leads out to the Military Road. The Vallum can be seen very plainly and the Roman road crosses its north bank and runs along it for a distance. As the access road leads towards the Milecastle Inn, the site of the fort of Haltwhistle Burn can be picked out overlooking the stream to the west. The fort was situated on the Stanegate and covered an area of three-quarters of an acre. Excavations showed that it had stone buildings, but these were demolished when the forts were transferred to the line of the Wall. In this area can be picked out several temporary forts or camps, probably used when the Romans were constructing the Wall. These are shown on the Ordnance Survey Map.

Great Chesters fort (Aesica) is reached by the farm road, which leaves the Military Road to the west of Haltwhistle Burn. It is nearly six miles from Housesteads and situated on an elevated site. It was intended to guard the Caw Gap and was smaller than Housesteads, covering between three and four acres. Like Housesteads it is entirely behind the Wall and the longer axis is from east to west. The farm house is beyond the east wall of the fort, but farm buildings occupy the north-east corner and the garden the eastern sector. Roman stone has been used in the reconstructed walls and it must be unusual to have a garden within a Roman fort. Excavations have taken place at various times, but the remains have not been consolidated and the fort is in a ruinous state. Only part of the vault of the strong room remains and the angle towers have suffered dilapidation. There could be very considerable remains if the fort were taken over and consolidated by the Department of Environment.

The approach road taken by the visitor follows the line of the Roman road from the Stanegate and crosses the Vallum on lower ground. There is a sharp slope to the fort, the defensive effect of which is spoilt by a field wall. Only at the south-east corner can the full height be realized.

The west tower of the south gate when excavated in 1894 revealed the famous hoard of jewellery including a gold brooch shaped like a hare, a silver collar with pendant and the much illustrated Aesica gold brooch, which is a masterpiece of Celtic art. Much of the stone has been removed, but the east guard-room contains an altar. Within the interior the foundations of some of the buildings remain exposed. The south ditch and Wall are prominent from the gate to the angle tower. The west wall stands up fairly high and against it a series of buildings have been constructed – it is not certain to what extent they were Roman, and further investigations are needed. The west gate has been blocked completely – it was reduced to one portal and then finally blocked. The masonry has not been removed by excavation and so this presents an unusual situation, showing alterations of four or five different periods. A building inscription of Hadrian from here was placed in Chesters Museum.

Beyond the west wall is a series of four parallel embankments. This was the weakest side of the fort and these have been proved to be very early in date. Excavations have shown that Milecastle 43 had been built on the Broad foundation. Then the change was made to the Narrow Wall and the milecastle, which could not be fitted into the building of the fort, was demolished. The four embankments pre-dated the building of the Narrow Wall.

The Wall can be traced westwards towards Allolee and Walltown Crags can be seen. There are extensive views in all directions. South of the fort was a civilian settlement. The bath-house was excavated in 1897 and there are traces of cultivation terraces to the west as at Housesteads. An interesting feature is a winding aqueduct, constructed to bring a supply of water to the fort from the Haltwhistle Burn. This is shown on the Ordnance Survey Map for a distance of about six miles.

To the west of the fort the Vallum repays a visit – it is situated at the bottom of the slope and in the area below Cockmount Hill farmhouse there are a number of crossings in a complete state with corresponding gaps in the mounds. The Vallum ditch was not cleaned out again and so it is possible to obtain from here a complete profile.

From Great Chesters it is possible to continue to follow the Wall or to return to the road and travel by car to the right turn to Walltown Quarries. Another turn right finds a farm road which goes back beyond the quarries and parking space can be found.

At Cockmount Hill Wood the Broad foundation and the Narrow Wall converge — from Greatchesters to this point the Narrow Wall had been built on a separate foundation. Turret 43b is west of the wood and further west near Allolee farmhouse, Milecastle 44 is very distinct. A good section of Wall is here, but by the farm only the core remains. We now reach the *Nine Nicks of Thirlwall*, rugged crags that have been reduced to seven by quarrying. The Wall climbs the crags and forms re-entrants. On the low ground the ditch has been cut. There is considerable limestone quarrying and there are dilapidated lime-kilns in the area. The writer has observed visitors taking note of these under the mistaken impression that they were turrets of the Roman Wall. Turrets 44 and 44b are on top of the crags. Walltown Nick is wide and rocky. The Wall is constructed straight across the lowest part, protected by the ditch. Hereabouts is a spring called *"King Arthur's Well"* and Walltown farmhouse is largely built of Roman stone. So are the walls and buildings. John Ridley's tower has probably been embodied in one of these, and the old village of Walltown has disappeared. The Wall climbs the crag westwards to Milecastle 45, and there is a fine stretch of it until quarrying is responsible for removing a large section. Then follows what is perhaps the best piece of the Wall — some 400 yards of it and Turret 45a are under the protection of the Department of Environment. The turret was an isolated signal station before it was embodied in the Wall system. Here are exciting views and it is possible to examine the structure of the Wall which has been exposed down to the Broad foundation. It shows the skill of the Roman engineers in straddling the crags with their defensive works. The present Greenhead quarry brings the Wall to an end, but fortunately there is to be no further destruction.

Beyond the smoking quarry, Greenhead can be seen and the line of the Wall as it continues westwards towards Gilsland.

The fort of **Carvoran,** approached by a farm drive, was situated on the Stanegate at its junction with the Maiden Way from the south — a place of great strategic importance. Carvoran is situated behind the Wall and the Vallum and guards the Tipalt valley. In Hadrian's time it was occupied by Hamian archers. It measures 440 feet by 360 feet, covering three and a half acres. The north-west angle is visible, but very few other remains, and it has not yet been excavated. Many important finds have been casual, like the famous corn measure now at Chesters. There was an external bath-house, a civilian settlement and a cemetery, all producing evidence. Carvoran has been acquired by the Vindolanda Trust.

Much of the stone has gone into farm buildings and beyond Carvoran the Wall disappears completely, though the Wall ditch is very plain. An examination of Thirlwall Castle, north of the Wall and overlooking the Tipalt Burn, shows where the Roman Wall has gone. Cartloads of finely cut Roman stone were taken to build a fortification of a later age.

The river, the road and the railway all cut through the gap made by the Tipalt. To the west of the road leaving Greenhead for Gilsland can be detected *Glenwelt Leazes Camp* close to the Stanegate. A small section of the Wall appears in the west bank above the road and the Vallum is also visible. Between Wallend and Chapel House the Wall ditch is very wide. About a quarter of a mile east of Chapel House is a section of Wall and it was built by the Twentieth Legion in Hadrian's time. The Vallum appears to the west and beyond the Poltross Burn Throp fort overlooks the Stanegate. At Poltross Burn the railway cuts across the line of the Wall and keeps close to Stanegate.

Poltross Burn Milecastle (48) is approached by a path near the railway station. The Burn, which divides Northumberland and Cumberland here, has carved a deep gorge and the railway has to cross by a viaduct, the tall arch of which would please the spirits of Roman Wall builders. The railway, however, obscures the significance of the site and Roman material has been removed to allow its passage. The milecastle has been very well preserved by the Department of Environment. The Roman road here obtrudes on to the Vallum. The milecastle measures seventy by sixty-one feet and all its walls were laid to the full breadth. This extends to twelve feet on either side of the milecastle. The north gate through the Wall had been reduced from ten feet to a single four feet door. Just within this is a structure of masonry with steps to the rampart, which it has been calculated was twelve feet, and parapet above. There are two barrack blocks – one on each side of the milecastle. There are the remains of ovens in the north-west corner. The ruins here are very impressive and the continuation of the Wall can be seen beyond the railway to the west. A fine stretch passes through the garden of the former vicarage. This provides a very good example of Narrow Wall built on Broad foundation.

Along the Brampton Road a gate opposite the school and the old vicarage leads to the next stretch of Wall and the Vallum comes very close. The Department of Environment has carried out some fine work of recovery and preservation. The Wall is Narrow on Broad foundation and this is easily investigated. Turret 48a has wing walls of the full width, showing how the turrets were built before the Wall which was completed with reduced width. Immediately west of the turret the River Irthing has encroached, washing away the Wall ditch and the Wall itself. Stones lie tumbled in the waters which move urgently and noisily on. There is a very considerable drop from the Wall to the river.

The next stage presents a remarkable surprise. The farm gate is in a break of the Wall and the farm approach follows the deep cavity of the Vallum. The Wall at one point stands to fourteen courses high. I remember this when it was completely overgrown and carried a large hedge. This has been removed and the Wall exposed to Willowford Farm. Here stands Turret 48b and visitors pay the farmer for permission to proceed, and this very fine stretch of Wall continues down the slope to **Willowford Bridge.** This is a situation very similar to that of Chesters – the Wall had to be carried over the river.

Here was another fine piece of engineering and the Romans again made use of harnessed water for driving a mill. The masonry is tumbled and rather complicated, but it seems that the bridge carried only the Wall over the river, but at a later stage it was widened and there was considerable reconstruction. A large tower was built against the Narrow Wall, which was built on Broad foundation. This tower replaced an earlier turret and both guarded the bridge abutment. There was some massive masonry used in the process of construction and to the north of the Wall was a stone apron or defence at river level to prevent erosion. The extended pier beyond the abutment was so constructed that a narrowing of the stone channel provided extra power for the undershot wheel of the water mill. A stone spindle-bearing of this still remains. The river is now considerably removed from its course in Roman times, so that the other piers of the bridge are completely covered. The erosion accounts for the very steep slope to the west of the river from which the Wall has disappeared. At the top is *Harrow Scar Milecastle* (49). This measures seventy-five feet from north to south and sixty-five feet from east to west. A farm lane cuts through it and it seems that the interior has been used for farm buildings. The south gate was reduced in size in Roman times. Excavation showed a turf milecastle on the site. The stone Wall proceeds westwards on a slightly different alignment to join the north wall of the fort of Birdoswald.

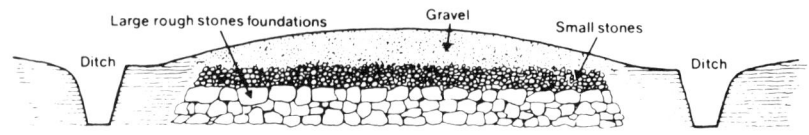

Large rough stones foundations   Gravel   Small stones

Ditch   Ditch

Cross section of Roman Road.

Birdoswald (Camboglanna – meaning Crooked Glen) overlooks the River Irthing and is situated in Cumberland. It is another magnificent situation with the winding river far beneath. Eastwards Walltown Crags are prominent and westwards on a fine day Burnswalk in Scotland can be picked out. The wastes of Spadeadam are to the north and the village of Moscow is not far away. There is a very fine stretch of the stone Wall eastwards from the fort, which continues to Harrow Scar Milecastle. From this point Willowford bridge can be seen below, with a further length of the Wall leading to Gilsland. The whole site is particularly impressive and the Wall here is well preserved. The line of the old turf Wall, which was constructed originally, can be seen to the south of the stone Wall. So there is a great deal in the area.

The fort is approached through the farm which is built within the fort and largely from Roman stone. The turf Wall left the usual area of the fort to the north, but when the stone Wall was built it was aligned to the north wall of the fort. The present entrance to the farm is by the rounded north-west corner of the fort, with an angle turret within which at a later time ovens were built. The masonry here is particularly good. The Wall proceeds to the south of the road, so that a fair stretch of it is preserved. It is all Narrow Wall since it was built later.

Beyond the farm the whole outline of the fort is revealed. The walls and gateways have been uncovered, but very little of the interior is visible except the wall of a granary that has become the retaining wall of the farm garden. The uneven turf shows considerable remains to uncover, the whole of the area being five acres. It could take 1,000 infantry or 500 cavalry.

Bewcastle some six miles to the north provided an early warning system. Here was situated an outpost fort. Birdoswald itself guarded the way to the north as well as the lateral route behind the Wall. The Stanegate was on the other side of the Irthing.

The Romans at Birdoswald took over a native fort and established a camp containing tents. Turrets were first erected for communication purposes in Agricola's time. In 122 in Hadrian's time the turf Wall and ditch were constructed. The ditch helped to provide material for the Wall and sections now still show the cut turf as it was piled up.

There were timber buildings on the site before the stone fort was constructed. The ditch had to be filled in and the Wall levelled in the area of the fort — the east and west gates of the fort were on this line. The fort was constructed according to the usual pattern, except that the granaries were aligned east and west instead of north and south. The walls of the fort were backed with earth and one soldier lost his bronze arm purse in the process. It was discovered in 1948 and contained twenty-eight Roman denarii of silver. These are now in Carlisle Museum together with thirty others found in a pot. They help to date the building of the fort to Hadrian's time.

It was intended as a cavalry fort, but by change of plan was converted to infantry. The stone Wall was now constructed to bring it into alignment with the north wall of the fort and a new ditch was cut. The turf wall was demolished on either side of this deviation, together with its turrets. This has provided interesting evidence on the turf Wall, which joins the stone Wall at *Wall Bowers Milecastle*.

Lea Hill Turret (51b) is an example of a turf Wall turret embodied in the stone Wall.

The reconstruction of Birdoswald Fort depicts it in 130 A.D. There is one slight error.

These two illustrations show the original turf wall of the fort and the later wall of stone.

Birdoswald has the curious interest of an intended cavalry fort with five gates south of the Wall and one through it. Its long axis is north-south, unlike Housesteads which is east-west.

Later in Hadrian's time the Vallum was cut and a crossing left opposite the south gate. The Vallum was filled in at a date not too distant – there was hardly enough room for it on the site. The Hadrianic fort suffered severe damage in A.D. 197 and the Emperor Severus had to reconstruct it. Very little Hadrianic material remains. Inscribed stones are mainly after A.D. 200. Severus built over Hadrianic foundations.

About A.D. 296 there was another disaster on the Wall, followed by further rebuilding. Different periods of rebuilding can be seen on the south wall of the fort. One of the best pieces of reconstruction of the third century is the East Gate, which was redesigned before it was repaired. The central piers were strengthened and the north portal's passageway was blocked to create a new room. The west entrance to the guardroom under the north tower was also blocked.

The Narrow Wall continues from the north-west corner of Birdoswald on the south of the road as far as Turret 49b, part of which remains. The road then obliterates the Wall, but the Wall ditch continues to the north. Across the field to the south the line of the turf Wall can be detected. First comes the turf Wall ditch, then the turf Wall about twenty feet wide and south of this the Vallum, which comes very close. The site of Milecastle 50 (High House), constructed later on the stone Wall, can be picked out but the turrets have disappeared. Excavation on these three sites, however, proved they were of Hadrianic construction, so that the turf Wall and stone Wall were both Hadrianic. They are separate from Birdoswald to Milecastle 51 where they converge, so this is an important section to investigate. At a barn called Appletree, near Turret 50b, a farm drive leads down to a point where the turf Wall can be seen in section. Part of the original turf is exposed and the Wall ditch, the turf Wall and the Vallum are very evident to the east of the drive, where the crossings can also be picked out. To the west beyond the stream and the trees the turf Wall and Vallum can be seen in the direction of Wallbowers, where turf and stone Walls join. The Vallum continues parallel to the stone Wall at a respectful distance.

It has been shown that the turf Wall continued westwards, by the fact that turf Wall turrets have been included in the stone Wall – the Wall was built up to the turrets and not bonded with them. The first to be seen in the excavated bank to the north of the road is *Piper Sike Turret* 51a. It stands six courses high and was built by the Twentieth Legion. The Narrow Wall abuts on to it. Inside was a large stone platform used as a living and sleeping area. To the south of the road in Coombe Wood was a large freestone quarry which was used by the Romans and inscriptions left by Roman soldiers on the rock have been discovered. Three – Securus, Justus and Maternus–

are considered genuine, another is thought to be a forgery of a much later date.

Lea Hill Turret 51b next emerges on the north bank of the road standing eight courses high. This was also a turf Wall turret, twenty feet square, i.e. the width of the turf Wall. On either side can be seen the straight join when the Narrow stone Wall was built. It was set back a little from the north front of the turret and the berm between Wall and ditch was very narrow.

Milecastle 52 **(Bankshead)** has provided two altars to Cocidius, a local god, which were taken to Lanercost. Excavation showed it to be a large milecastle, measuring seventy-seven feet from north to south and ninety feet from east to west internally. This is explained by the fact that at Pike Hill, a little to the west, was a signal tower, twenty feet square, and so extra men were needed. The Department of Environment have exposed one angle of this to the south of the road. It includes the doorway and a considerable amount of pottery was found. Contact could be made with Gillalees Beacon on the Bewcastle road.

A short distance westwards is East Banks Turret 52a. This, together with a length of the Wall, has been preserved by the Department of Environment. The turret is a very good example of the turf Wall type and the Narrow stone Wall is built up to it on either side. Part of the masonry of the turret has fallen, but it stands twelve courses high and projects a foot to the north of the Wall. There is a plinth after five courses. The door is to the south and there are the remains of a living platform within. There is a fine piece of modern stone walling by local craftsmen to the south of the car park. The ditch is on the north side of the road, and a lime kiln stands square like a turret to a height of twenty feet. It has a fine pointed arch and is mistaken for Roman since it is so prominent. There are very fine views of the Irthing valley and a farmhouse at **Banks** is being converted into a Museum and Gallery by Li Yuan Chia – hence the L.Y.C. Museum. "It is hoped that the collections exhibited will include Roman and British antiquities and Cumbrian folk art and the works of international artists".

Beyond Banks village it is worth taking the road north to **Bewcastle,** seven miles away, the site of an important outpost fort. It has the interest that there is a medieval castle built of Roman stone within the Roman fort, and the church with its famous carved Anglo-Saxon Cross. The Inn is called the "Kiln".

The fort covers an area of six acres and is hexagonal in shape. The ramparts on the south and west are very pronounced and unevenness of the ground within indicates the foundations of Roman barracks. Excavations in 1937 revealed the headquarters buildings and part of the commandant's house. A Roman road linked the fort with Birdoswald. The road back to Banks passes *Askerton Castle,* an interesting structure dating back to the fifteenth century and belonging to the Dacres.

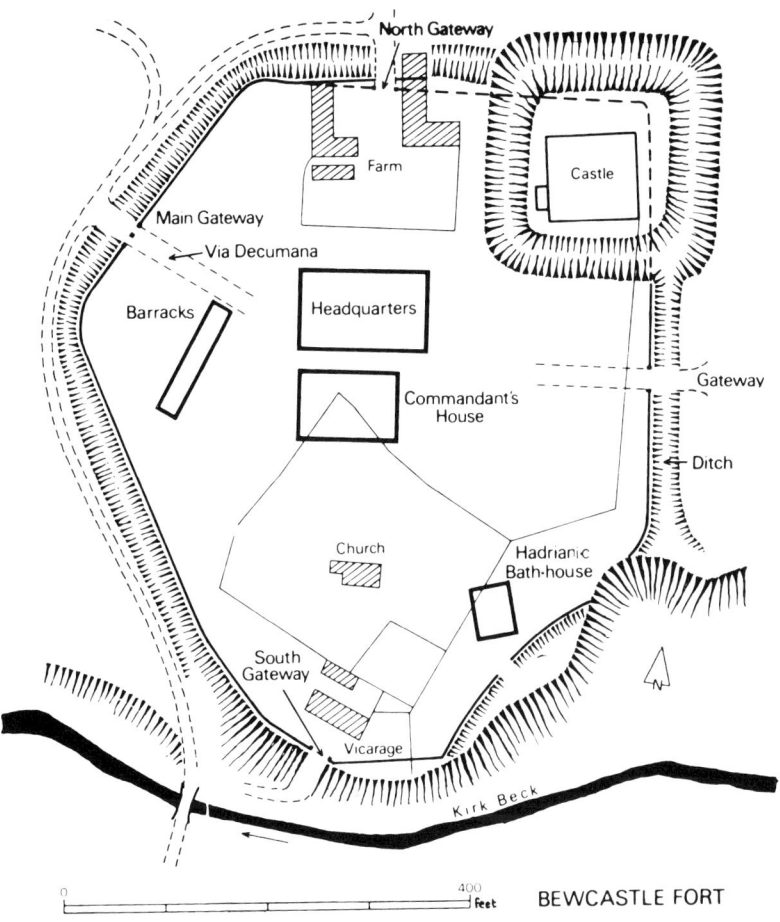

BEWCASTLE FORT

On returning to the line of the Wall at Banks Burn Farm was Milecastle 53 and to the west of it a small section of the Wall stands to a height of nearly ten feet. It is possible to follow the line of the Wall by footpath. The Wall itself has mostly disappeared, but the Wall ditch and the Vallum are both very pronounced. The Wall rises over Craggle Hill and falls to Haytongate, a deserted farmhouse which includes Roman stone. Hereabouts is the line of a geological fault known as the Red Rock Fault and to the west of this there is no limestone. Lanercost Priory lies in the valley below and for its construction the Roman Wall was extensively robbed. The building

41

Opposite: A Centurion and a Standard Bearer.

has curious coloration, since part of it is red rock and part whitish limestone. The nave of the church is used for parish purposes and the remains of the Abbey are under the guardianship of the Department of Environment. There are Roman stones in the museum.

Continuing along the Wall and after crossing the Burtholme Burn, a considerable stretch of masonry is visible underneath the roots of the trees and the hedge. Only the core remains and the cement contrasts with the red rock. North of the Stone Wall another stretch of the turf Wall can be seen as far as the road leading south from Garthside.

At Turret 54a hereabouts, some confusion was sorted out by excavation. It showed that the first turf Wall turret had collapsed and had to be built further south. It was later embodied in the stone Wall and obliterated by the rebuilding of Severus. The Wall here has become wider, but it has mostly disappeared. It can be vaguely traced by Howgill and Low Wall where there is a milecastle. It becomes a field bank covered with a lofty hedge and trees down to Dovecote Bridge. Here, after much searching, I found a stretch of the Wall beyond the bridge and below Walltown.

Milecastle 56 is under the southern limit of the village of Walltown and Roman stone can be seen in some of the buildings. The public house, once the Black Horse, is now called the Centurion. The Wall can next be picked out at Sandysike and the Vallum deviates south to take in the fort of **Castlesteads** (Uxellodunum). This overlooked the Cambeck valley but suffered from landscaping in the eighteenth century, when the present Castlesteads House was built. Excavations in 1934 traced the outline of the fort, which covered three and three-quarter acres. There was a turf and timber fort before the fort of stone. It is behind both the Cambeck and the Wall, situated something like a quarter of a mile from Milecastle 57. This is explained by landscape and strategy.

From Castlesteads it is worth making a visit to the Stanegate fort at **Old Church, Brampton.** It is approached by a narrow lane called Old Church Lane, north of Brampton and near the Secondary School, in the grounds of which were uncovered a number of kilns for the making of pottery and tiles. The fort is situated on higher ground above the River Irthing, which erodes the red rock and earth. The unusual feature about the fort is that at least one third of the area is occupied by the Church of St. Martin and a well-filled cemetery. The headquarters buildings and some of the barracks have been identified in the field to the south and the perimeter of the fort is marked by a high mound, on which grow ancient ash trees. The rampart was of turf, but the buildings were of stone. The connection with the Stanegate can be seen as a deep cutting.

The continuation of the line of the Wall is not easy to discover, since the stonework has disappeared and there is no road keeping close to the line continuously. By crossing the river to Irthington, the site of Milecastle 58 can be detected near Newtown and west of White Flat the remains of the Wall form a field boundary. The Wall and the Vallum are here very close together. Milecastle 59 takes the name of the farm "Old Wall", appropriately since the buildings contain a lot of Roman stone. The Wall is shown by the ditch continuing to *High Strand* (Milecastle 60), and then in turn as revealed by place-names to *Wallhead* (Milecastle 61), *Walby East* (Milecastle 62) and *Walby West* (Milecastle 63); Milecastle 64 was near Drawdikes Castle.

The River Eden now comes close to the south of the Wall.

The modern military depot has been named Hadrian's Camp. The line of the Wall continues south-west towards **Stanwix,** now a northern suburb of Carlisle and very much built upon. The extent of the fort has been traced and it measured 580 feet from north to south and 700 feet from east to west, enclosing more than nine acres. It provided quarters for a cavalry regiment 1,000 strong and was the largest fort on the Wall. It was called Petriana.

The south-west rampart can be detected in the corner of the churchyard and the site of a granary was discovered during the extension of the school playground. Various Roman relics have been discovered including tombstones and bronze articles. The Museum of Tullie House at Carlisle on the other side of the Eden is the repository for local relics and is well worth a visit.

Carlisle was the largest settlement in the Roman Wall area and though little of it remains the ruins of Corstopitum can give some impression of its appearance. Evidence of an Agricolan fort of timber has been discovered — one side of it at considerable depth under Tullie House. It seems that a firm basis was provided by great timber platforms since part of the area was very wet and these rafts carried the structure. A civilian settlement grew up near the fort containing shops, houses and taverns. It was called **Luguvalium.**

The army transferred to the Wall, north of the river, to the fort of Stanwix and Carlisle became entirely civilian. Very little is known about the buildings, but various ornaments, pieces of pottery, coins, inscribed stones, altars and grave slabs have been found. Bede talks of Cuthbert's visit to the town, mentioning its walls and "the remarkable fountain, formerly built by the Romans". The Roman areas have been completely covered by more modern building and much is left to the imagination.

From Stanwix and Carlisle a Roman road led to the outpost fort of Netherby on the Esk, where there are no visible remains. On the Eden, west of Stanwix, was Milecastle 66, which overlooked the river crossing. Stones of the bridge were recovered from the river in 1951. The Wall crossed the area of the Sewage Works and stones located in 1931 were removed to Tullie House. Beyond Stainton (Milecastle 67) a short section of the Vallum is visible, coming very close to the river. It then goes directly to Kirkandrews, whereas the Wall keeps closer to the river, reaching Grinsdale. Here the Wall ditch is visible and Milecastle 69 was to the west. Wall and Vallum come close again at Kirkandrews and then separate. The Vallum goes direct to the fort of Burgh-by-Sands, whereas the Wall goes north to

Beaumont and then turns westwards.

The fort of **Burgh by Sands** (Aballa) covered nearly five acres. It was intended to guard the Solway fords hereabouts. There was also a Roman civilian settlement. The fort projected beyond the Wall and its stones were used in buildings of the later village. The church itself, which stands within the fort area, contains a good deal of Roman stone. The bath-house was destroyed in the cutting of the Carlisle canal. This in turn became the route of the railway and now the railway has been closed. Too little care was taken with the Roman remains, but the church tower is a good example of the border type of pele tower. Roman stones were re-used for a similar purpose.

There is a monument to Edward I, 'hammer of the Scots', who died near here in 1307. He reminds us of the Roman Emperor Severus, who had parts of the Wall rebuilt and died at York in A.D. 211. Edward's monument is on the edge of the salt marshes of the Solway, and the Wall continues to the small fort of **Drumburgh.** It covered two acres and first had clay ramparts, before being built in stone. Most of the stone was taken by Thomas, Lord Dacre, in the time of Henry VIII, for the purpose of building his castle, a "prety pyle". It is now ruinous, but provided a very suitable site for surveying the Solway and the Scottish territory beyond.

The Wall as a grassy mound can be seen to the west of Drumburgh and crosses the old railway to reach Milecastle 77 at Glasson. The Vallum is also visible and comes close to the Wall at Milecastle 78. Turret 78b was on the site of Port Carlisle. The harbour was built by the Earl of Lonsdale in 1819 and a canal to connect it with Carlisle was opened in 1823, but it did not flourish.

The Wall can be detected as far as Bowness and Milecastle 79 (Solway House) was excavated for the Pilgrimage of 1949. The stone Wall milecastle covered the site of a slightly smaller turf Wall milecastle, giving further proof that the turf Wall continued right across to **Bowness on Solway,** the last of the Wall forts.

It stands on a sea cliff, fifty feet high, overlooking the last ford on the estuary, which widens to the Irish Sea, and is subject to fitful tides which have been fatal to travellers, fishermen and wild fowlers. Raiders took advantage of low tides. The Roman fort (called **Maia**) was large, covering seven acres. The north wall was lost by erosion to the sea, but the south wall was located by excavation to the north of the church, which was built of Roman stone. The baths have been located and the line of the west ditch. Milecastle 80 was covered by the fort and earlier writers have indicated that the Wall continued beyond the fort to the water as at Wallsend. The Roman Wall completed its eighty Roman miles from Tyne to Solway, but this was not the end of Roman fortifications. The Solway could be crossed by boat and the Romans had to construct further forts at Beckfoot, Maryport, Burrow Walls and Moresby. There were fortlets at every mile, and turrets in between, but there was not the continuous barrier of the Wall.

The Aesica Brooch

Our illustration
is the size of
the original

This magnificent statue is probably of Cybele.

List of Roman Monuments in the care of English Heritage

Standard Hours of Admission	Mid March to Mid October	Mid October to Mid March
Monday – Saturday	9.30 – 18.30	9.30 – 16.00
Sunday	14.00 – 18.30	14.00 – 16.00

A— Any reasonable time   X— Admission free
P— Parking facilities   T— Toilets   S— Standard hours
SM — Sunday mornings from 9.30 a.m. — April to September.

Northumberland	Hours	O.S. Map ref. 1:50,000
X Roman Wall at Benwell (Condercum), Newcastle upon Tyne	A	88 NZ 215646
X Roman Wall at Benwell Roman Temple, Newcastle upon Tyne	A	88 NZ 217646
X Roman Wall at Denton Hall Turret, Newcastle upon Tyne	A	88 NZ 198655
X Roman Wall at West Denton, Newcastle upon Tyne	A	88 NZ 195656
X Roman Wall at Heddon-on-the-Wall To Portgate	A	88 NZ 136669
PT Corbridge (Corstopitum) Roman Station	S	87 NY 983649
X Roman Wall at Planetrees Farm, Chollerford	A	87 NY 928696
X Roman Wall at Brunton Turret, Chollerford	A	87 NY 921698
X Roman Wall at Chesters Bridge Abutment, Chollerford	A	87 NY 914700
PT Roman Wall at Chesters (Cilurnum)		87 NY 913701
Roman Fort Chollerford	S SM	
Roman Wall at Black Carts	A	87 NY 884712
PX Roman Wall at Carrawburgh, Temple of Mithras	A	87 NY 869713
X Roman Wall at Sewingshields, Haydon Bridge	A	87 NY 813702
PT Roman Wall at Housesteads (Bercovicium) Roman Fort, Bardon Mill	S SM	87 NY 790687
PX Roman Wall at Chesterholm (Vindolanda) Roman Fort and Milestone, Bardon Mill	S	87 NY 771664
PX Roman Wall at Winshields Milecastle, Bardon Mill	A	87 NY 745676
Roman Wall at Cawfields	A	87 NY 726669
X Roman Wall at Walltown Crags, Greenhead	A	87 NY 674664

Cumbria	Hours	O.S. Map ref. 1:50,000
PX Roman Wall at Poltross Burn Milecastle, Gilsland	*A*	86 NY 634662
X Roman Wall at Gilsland (garden of Roman Way guest house)	*A*	86 NY 631662
X Roman Wall at Willowford Bridge Abutment, Gilsland	*A*	86 NY 629664
X Roman Wall at Harrow's Scar Milecastle, Gilsland	*A*	86 NY 621664
Roman Wall at Birdoswald Fort (Camboglanna), Gilsland (Admission to the walls of the fort is controlled by the tenant farmer.)	*A*	86 NY 615663
X Roman Wall at Piper Sike Turret, Brampton	*A*	86 NY 588654
X Roman Wall at Leahill Turret, Brampton	*A*	86 NY 585653
X Roman Wall at Banks East Turret, Brampton	*A*	86 NY 579648
Roman Wall at Pike Hill Turret	*A*	86 NY 577648
X Roman Wall at Banks Hill, nr. Walton	*A*	86 NY 568645

Museums:

South Shields, Roman Fort Museum   88 NZ 365679

Open		Tuesday – Friday	10.00 – 17.30
		Saturday	10.00 – 16.30
	Easter – October	Sunday	14.00 – 17.00

Newcastle, Museum of Antiquities   88 NZ 247650

Open	Monday – Saturday	10.00 – 17.00

Carlisle, Tullie House Museum   85 NY 399559

Open	April – September	Monday – Saturday	9.00 – 17.00
	Mid June – Mid September	Sunday	10.00 – 16.00

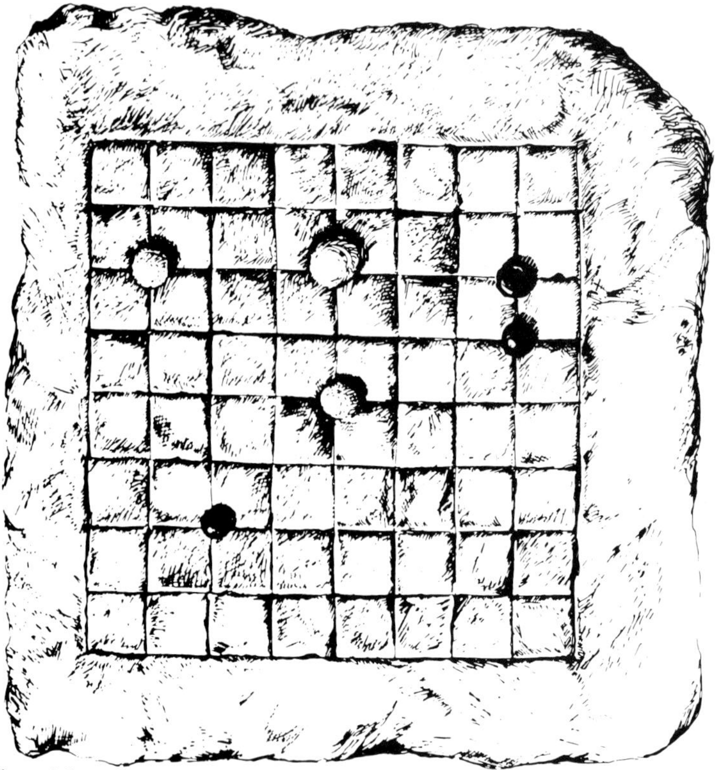

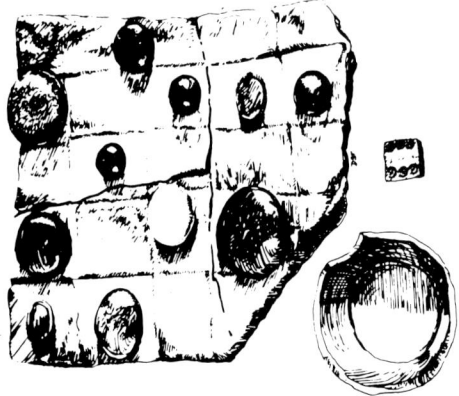

The soldiers on the Wall played many games to pass the time during monotonous periods off duty. One game was the *ludus latrunculorum* (a *latro* was a mercenary soldier), the ancestor of the present-day game of draughts. At Corbridge a collection of glass game pieces — *latrones* — was found, as well as several boards. The pieces seem to have moved like rooks in chess and the aim was to capture the enemy pieces by trapping one between two of your own.

Stone Gaming Board with counters, dice and dice box found at Vindolanda.